S0-BBC-712

THE TECH BEHIND

AMPHIBIOUS VEHICLES

by Steve Goldsworthy

CAPSTONE PRESS
a capstone imprint

Edge Books are published by Capstone Press,
1710 Roe Crest Drive, North Mankato, Minnesota 56003
www.capstonepub.com

Library of Congress Cataloging-in-Publication Data
Names: Goldsworthy, Steve, author.
Title: The tech behind amphibious vehicles / by Steve Goldsworthy.
Other titles: Technology behind amphibious vehicles
Description: North Mankato, Minnesota : Capstone Press,
   2020. | Series: Edge books. tech on wheels |
   Audience: Ages 8-14. | Audience: Grades 7-8.
Identifiers: LCCN 2018060562|
ISBN 9781543573060 (hardcover) | ISBN 9781543573107 (ebook pdf)
Subjects: LCSH: Motor vehicles, Amphibious--Juvenile literature.
Classification: LCC TL235.63 .G65 2020 | DDC 629.2--dc23
LC record available at https://lccn.loc.gov/2018060562

Editorial Credits
Carrie Braulick Sheely, editor; Jennifer Bergstrom, designer; Eric Gohl, media researcher;
Katy LaVigne, production specialist

Photo Credits
Alamy: Conner Flecks, 26; AP Photo: Carlos Osorio, 10; DVIDS: U.S. Marine Corps, 17,
U.S. Marine Corps/Lance Cpl. Immanuel Johnson, 9; iStockphoto: dan_prat, 24; Newscom:
Reuters/Denis Balibouse, 18, Reuters/Steve Marcus, 8, Supplied by WENN.com, 4, 16,
ZUMA Press/Chris Crewell, 22, ZUMA Press/Courtesy Rinspeed, 29, Zuma Press/Gary
Lee, 14, ZUMA Press/Gibbs Sports, cover; Shutterstock: Fouad A. Saad, 13, Sergey D, 12;
Wikimedia: Public Domain, 7, Tyg728, 20

Design Elements: Shutterstock

Printed in and bound in the USA.
PA70

The technology in today's recreational amphibious vehicles helps them move through the water easily.

CHAPTER 1

OVER LAND AND ACROSS WATER

A flashy car zooms down a beautiful, sandy beach. It heads straight for the ocean with no signs of stopping. Splash! The car drives right into the water and keeps going! It is one of the latest amphibious vehicle designs.

From sporty cars to powerful military vehicles, companies are making amphibious vehicles in all shapes and sizes. Some of the newest, sleekest designs get a lot of attention. But they don't just look cool from the outside. Each vehicle is loaded with cutting-edge tech.

Early Days

The history of amphibious vehicles goes back to before the first cars hit the streets in the early 1900s. In the early days of logging, companies had to haul logs across muddy swamps and shallow streams. In 1878, Canadian businessman Joseph Jackson asked the West and Peachey company to help make this job easier. The company's steam-powered Alligator Tug became the first successful amphibious vehicle. Side-mounted paddle wheels pushed it along in the water. A cable winch pulled it across land.

winch—a machine that can wind and unwind a cable to help pull heavy objects

Other companies soon began designing amphibious vehicles that could operate better. Most of these early vehicles combined a car chassis with a boat hull. It took many years to get the design right.

In 1931, American Peter Prell created one of the first successful amphibious cars. His "land-boat" had a boat-like hull. It moved on tracks instead of wheels. The vehicle reached speeds of 40 miles (64 kilometers) per hour on land and 25 miles (40 km) per hour on water. Prell built just one for himself, but his invention got a lot of attention. It inspired others to build their own versions.

The United States, Great Britain, and Germany created military amphibious vehicles during World War II (1939–1945). The British DUKW had a hollow, airtight body. It moved on wheels on land. A propeller powered it through water. The German Volkswagen Schwimmwagen was also called a "bucket car." The small wheeled vehicle had a propeller at the back. The propeller could fold up when the vehicle was on land. The Schwimmwagen's hull had no doors. Users climbed in and out.

A DUKW carries troops and supplies across a river in the Netherlands during World War II.

chassis—the frame on which the body of a vehicle is built

hull—the frame or body of a ship

propeller—a rotating blade that moves a vehicle through water

Designers used very different tech in the modern WaterCar Panther (left) than they did in the Amphicar from the 1960s (right).

CHAPTER 2

CUTTING-EDGE TECH

Amphibious vehicles have come a long way since the early days. Designers have spent years testing ideas and parts. From lighter, stronger body materials to retractable wheels, today's cutting-edge tech is a result of their hard work. Today recreational amphibious vehicles are available for people to buy. Militaries around the world use hovercraft and other amphibious vehicles.

The AAV7AI has a ship-like hull design that angles up at the front.

Body Design and Hydrodynamics

The body is a key part of amphibious vehicle design. Designers must consider hydrodynamics. Streamlined bodies help a vehicle move through the water efficiently.

Most amphibious vehicles use hull designs similar to ships and boats. The main Amphibious Assault Vehicle (AAV) of the U.S. Marine Corps is the AAV7AI. The front of its wide hull angles upward like a ship hull to help it move through the water.

hovercraft—a vehicle that travels on a cushion of air over both land and water

hydrodynamics—a branch of science that deals with the motion of fluids and how objects move through fluids

retractable—able to draw back or inside

Some recreational amphibious vehicles act like speedboats. The front of the WaterCar Panther slopes upward to a point just under the bumper. This design pushes the water to the sides of the vehicle. The Gibbs Biski has a body design like a jet ski. Its thin, pointed front helps it cut through the water.

The wheels of the Quadski fold up into its body.

Amphibious vehicle designers also consider drag. Wheels or external engine parts that drag through the water can slow down the vehicle. Some amphibious vehicles have retractable wheels to prevent drag. When the Gibbs Quadski hits the water, the driver touches a button. Two small motors then lift the four wheels of the all-terrain vehicle (ATV) into the body. The motors push the wheels back down when the vehicle moves back on land.

FACT
The Quadski's wheels will not retract unless it is in at least 3 feet (0.9 meter) of water.

all-terrain vehicle—a vehicle with four large wheels that travels easily over rough ground; these vehicles are also called ATVs

Flotation and Buoyancy

Designers have different ways of increasing a vehicle's buoyancy. Many amphibious vehicles use a simple tub-like design to float. As long as no water gets into the vehicle, it will act like a tub of air and float. Other vehicles use pontoon technology. This design uses airtight metal compartments filled with air inside the vehicle's body. The Sherp ATV has giant, air-filled tires to help it float. Each tire can hold about 210 gallons (800 liters) of air.

On land the Sherp's huge tires help it get through mud.

THE SCIENCE OF BUOYANCY

When an object goes in water, it moves away, or displaces, a certain amount of water. The water pushes up with a force equal to the weight of the displaced water. As long as the object weighs less than the water it displaces, it will float. The shape or size of an object doesn't determine buoyancy. For example, a large tub with a bunch of rocks can float as long as it weighs less than the water it displaces.

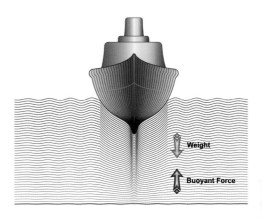

Weight

Buoyant Force

FACT

The Sherp's tires are more than 5 feet (1.5 m) tall. This is about the height of a monster truck's tires!

buoyancy—the tendency of an object to float or rise when submerged in a fluid

pontoon—a flat-bottomed boat that often has large, tube-shaped parts attached to its bottom to help it float

Waterproof Design

Regular cars are not designed to go in water. They have many of their mechanical parts exposed. A car's engine would easily flood in water and stop working. An amphibious vehicle needs a waterproof design that protects its mechanical parts. Many amphibious vehicles are designed as boats with wheels. For these vehicles, only the wheel compartments need to be sealed.

The Aquada has a frame that is bonded with aluminum. Its design keeps water out and prevents rust.

The Dutch Amphicruiser has a different design. It is a four-wheel drive vehicle that looks like a standard sport-utility vehicle (SUV). When it drives into the water, the bottom of the vehicle's doors are submerged. Designers added air-filled seals to the doors to keep the water out. The engine is enclosed in a watertight chamber. Underneath the chassis, the exhaust system and driveshaft are also sealed.

Most military amphibious vehicles have welded aluminum hulls. Manufacturers put a sealant along the seams where metal meets metal to avoid any leakage. This sealant is often made of silicone. Plastic coverings called O-ring seals are placed over any bolts to keep water out.

Body Material

In the past, many amphibious vehicles were made of steel, which rusts in water. Manufacturers sealed the vehicles with rust-resistant paint. Today most amphibious vehicles use modern materials that are much lighter and will not rust. For example, many recreational amphibious vehicles have fiberglass hulls and bodies.

The WaterCar Panther's chromoly frame is covered with a lightweight fiberglass body.

EXTREME TESTING

The U.S. Marine Corps has a department dedicated to testing amphibious vehicles. Its main focus is quality control and safety. Workers test everything from top speeds to endurance and buoyancy. They might run a vehicle nonstop for five days straight to test the engine. To test the vehicle's center of balance, they hang it from a giant crane. This will tell designers if a vehicle is likely to flip over in rough water. Once a vehicle passes these tests, it is considered safe and reliable for the Marines.

A new Marine Corps amphibious vehicle goes through tests in high waves.

The U.S. Marine Corps AAV7AI has a hull made of aluminum alloy. The main material in the hull is aluminum, but it also has other materials such as copper and silicon. This material is much stronger than fiberglass, but it's still lightweight.

The WaterCar Panther is built on a chromoly frame. Chromoly is lightweight yet strong. It is made of steel, chromium, and other materials. The car weighs less than 3,000 pounds (1,360 kilograms). Chromoly makes the car fast and helps it float well in the water.

alloy—a combination of two or more metals

fiberglass—a strong, lightweight material made from thin threads of glass

propeller

The Rinspeed Splash has a propeller at its rear to help power it through water.

CHAPTER 3

MOVING ON LAND AND WATER

Body design can make an amphibious vehicle look fast. But how a vehicle looks doesn't matter if it can't move well. Amphibious vehicles use some very cool tech to get going.

Moving Through Water

Some amphibious vehicles move through the water simply by spinning their wheels. These wheels have been fitted with paddle-like ridges. The Sherp has long, straight treads on its tires to propel the vehicle through water.

Other vehicles use screw-propellers like regular boats do. The motor turns the propeller at the back of the vehicle. The propeller pushes water behind it to move the vehicle forward.

The fastest amphibious vehicles use water jet propulsion. A water jet on the hull takes in water and forces it back out at a high speed. The backward rush of water pushes the vehicle forward. WaterCar claims its Panther is the fastest amphibious car in the world. The car's powerful jet propellers help it reach speeds up to 45 miles (72 km) in the water.

tread—a ridge on a tire

Driving on Land

Most amphibious vehicles operate like standard cars on land. Extra features can improve how the vehicles handle.

The ZBD-04 has a top speed of 40 miles (64 km) per hour on land.

Many amphibious vehicles have to travel across ice, snow, and mud. The giant tires on the Sherp can adjust to different types of surfaces. They can let our air to travel on loose or rough surfaces. They can add air to travel on firm roadways. The Chinese military's ZBD-04 tracked amphibious vehicle has six road wheels. Each wheel is fitted with shock absorbers to help smooth the ride over bumps. Drivers can also fit the metal tracks with rubber pads to improve handling over rocky ground. The WaterCar Panther acts like a four-wheel-drive jeep on land. Its off-road suspension can handle bumps.

FACT
In 2012, inventor Marc Witt built an amphibious car called the Sea Lion. It reached 125 miles (201 km) per hour on land.

suspension—the system of springs and shock absorbers that absorbs a car's up-and-down movements

A driver steers the Argo Bigfoot with levers.

CHAPTER 4

CONTROLLING AN AMPHIBIOUS VEHICLE

The way drivers control an amphibious vehicle depends on its propulsion system. Most amphibious vehicles have control features similar to those of boats and ships. A driver controls a propeller's turn with a steering wheel. The propeller then turns left or right.

Vehicles that use water jets often have a swivel attached to the bottom of the vehicle. This allows the jets to turn from side to side. The driver controls the angle of the water jets with a steering wheel. Underneath the hull, the water jets push the vehicle in the desired direction.

The Argo Bigfoot six-wheeler ATV uses two separate control levers to steer the vehicle. The wheels act like paddles. The left lever controls the left wheels. The right lever controls the right wheels. The wheels can move forward or backward. To turn, the driver can push forward on one lever and back on the other.

FACT
The small Gibbs Biski is like a combination of a motorcycle and a jet ski. It uses water jets and the weight of the driver's own body to turn.

swivel—a device joining two parts so that one or both can turn freely

Hovercraft

The hovercraft is a unique kind of amphibious vehicle. Hovercraft come in many sizes. Some are gigantic passenger ships. Others are one-person recreational vehicles. Whatever their size or use, they all use the same tech.

Fans at the back of a hovercraft push it forward over the water.

A hovercraft has a large rubber "skirt" under it. An engine powers fans. One powerful fan blows air down into the skirt. The fan creates a cushion of air for the hovercraft to float on. Other fans at the back of the craft push the vehicle forward or backward.

Controlling the direction of a hovercraft is similar to using a water jet. The only difference is that air moves the vehicle instead of water. The driver uses a steering wheel to control rudders at the hovercraft's rear. This angles the rudders, which changes the direction of air flow. The hovercraft then turns left or right.

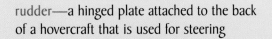

rudder—a hinged plate attached to the back of a hovercraft that is used for steering

The ACV's wheels will help it travel easily across deserts and many other types of terrain.

CHAPTER 5

THE FUTURE OF AMPHIBIOUS VEHICLES

Amphibious vehicles keep changing as designers come up with better materials, more powerful engines, and more efficient designs. The amphibious vehicles of the future will be faster and more versatile for both work and play.

The U.S. Marines are developing the Amphibious Combat Vehicle (ACV). The ACV is an eight-wheeled vehicle that will soon replace the current tracked AAVs. These wheels will give the ACV more speed and better steering control than the AAV7AIs. The ACV's powerful engine will produce 690 horsepower. In the water the vehicle will move about as fast as the AAV7AI's top speed of 8 miles (13 km) per hour. But on land it will reach speeds up to 65 miles (105 km) per hour. This is much faster than the current AAV7AI top land speed of 45 miles (72 km) per hour.

China is developing the VNI8 Amphibious Assault Vehicle. It can travel up to 40 miles (64 km) per hour by land and 19 miles (31 km) on water. These speeds will make it one of the fastest amphibious military vehicles in the world. The VNI8 AAV's tracks and wheels can retract into the body to reduce drag in water.

horsepower—a unit for measuring an engine's power

Ideas for the Future

How do designers come up with new concepts for amphibious vehicles? They use their imagination. They explore new technology or use old technology in a new way. Once they have a plan, they build a prototype. A prototype is a first model that other vehicles can be based on. Many of these prototypes are pretty radical.

Like something out of a spy film, the sQuba changes from a car on land to a submarine in water. It has an open roof. Drivers use scuba gear to breathe inside their car underwater.

An amphibious car of the future might look like the Amphi-X. This streamlined design uses both paddle wheels and water jets to move in the water.

The sQuba is an amphibious car that dives underwater.

Amphibious vehicles have come a long way from the early days. Creative designs and scientific advances have guided designers along the way. No matter what the future holds for amphibious vehicles, you can bet that cool new tech will be at the heart of it.

prototype—a first trial model of something made to test and improve the design

scuba—a device that uses a tank of compressed air that allows users to breathe underwater; scuba stands for self-contained underwater breathing apparatus all-terrain vehicle (AHL-tuh-RAYN VEE-uh-kuhl)—a vehicle with four large wheels that travels easily over rough ground

alloy (A-loy)—a combination of two or more metals

buoyancy (BOI-yuhn-see)—the tendency of an object to float or rise when submerged in a fluid

chassis (CHA-see)—the frame on which the body of a vehicle is built

fiberglass (FY-buhr-glas)—a strong, lightweight material made from thin threads of glass

hovercraft (HUHV-ur-kraft)—a vehicle that travels on a cushion of air over both land and water

horsepower (HORSS-pou-ur)—a unit for measuring an engine's power

hull (HUL)—the frame or body of a ship

hydrodynamics (hy-dro-dy-NAH-miks)—a branch of science that deals with the motion of fluids and how objects move through fluids

pontoon (pahn-TOON)—a flat-bottomed boat that often has large, tube-shaped parts attached to its bottom to help it float

propeller (pruh-PEL-ur)—a rotating blade that moves a vehicle through water

prototype (PROH-tuh-tipe)—a first trial model of something made to test and improve the design

retractable (ri-TRAKT-ay-buhl)—able to draw back or inside

rudder (RUHD-ur)—a hinged plate attached to the back of a hovercraft that is used for steering

scuba (SCOO-bah)—a device that uses a tank of compressed air that allows users to breathe underwater; scuba stands for self-contained underwater breathing apparatus

suspension (suh-SPEN-shuhn)—the system of springs and shock absorbers that absorbs a car's up-and-down movements

swivel (SWI-vuhl)—a device joining two parts so that one or both can turn freely

tread (TRED)—a ridge on a tire

winch (WINCH)—a machine that can wind and unwind a cable to help pull heavy objects

READ MORE

Bethea, Nikole Brooks. *High-Tech Highways and Super Skyways:
The Next 100 Years of Transportation.* Our World: The Next 100 Years.
North Mankato, MN: Capstone, 2017.

Burrows, Terry. *Hovercrafts and Humvees: Engineering Goes to War.*
STEM on the Battlefield. Minneapolis: Lerner, 2017.

Nagelhout, Ryan. *Amphibious Vehicles.* Mighty Military Machines.
New York: Gareth Stevens, 2016.

INTERNET SITES

Amphibious Assaults of World War II
https://www.history.com/topics/world-war-ii/amphibious-assaults-of-
world-war-ii-video

Christopher Cockerell: Hovercraft
https://www.geniusstuff.com/videos/41729-christopher-cockerell-
and-the-hovercraft-video.htm

How the sQuba Works
https://auto.howstuffworks.com/squba.htm